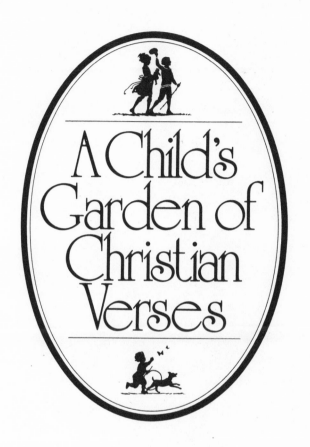

A Child's Garden of Christian Verses

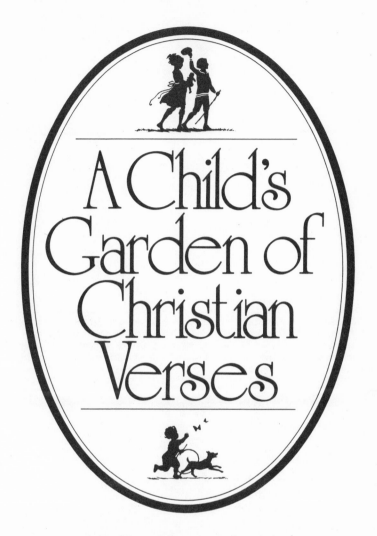

A Child's Garden of Christian Verses

Adapted from Robert Louis Stevenson by

K A T H R Y N   L I N D S K O O G

A Division of GL Publications
Ventura, CA U.S.A.

The foreign language publishing of all Regal books is under the direction of GLINT. GLINT provides financial and technical help for the adaptation, translation and publishing of books for millions of people worldwide. For more information regarding translation write: GLINT, P.O. Box 6688, Ventura, CA 93006.

Published by Regal Books
A Division of GL Publications
Ventura, California 93006
Printed in U.S.A.

Library of Congress Cataloging in Publication Data
Lindskoog, Kathryn.
    A child's garden of Christian verses.

    Summary: Adaptations of Stevenson's poems from a Christian point of view.
    1. Children's poetry, American.   2. Christian poetry, American.
[1. Christian life—Poetry 2. American Poetry] I. Stevenson, Robert Louis, 1850-1894. Child's garden of verses.   II. Title.
PS3562.I5125C45   1983   811'.54   83-9534
ISBN 0-8307-0890-1

Dedicated to Fay Blix

CONTENTS

INTRODUCTION

A century ago one superb children's book after another was being born: *Water Babies, Alice's Adventures in Wonderland, Hans Brinker, Little Women, Black Beauty, The Five Little Peppers and How They Grew, Tom Sawyer, Uncle Remus, The Princess and Curdie, Little Lord Fauntleroy,* and *Treasure Island.* At that very time the first great children's illustrators were producing books almost every year. Walter Crane (1845-1915), Kate Greenaway (1846-1901), and Ralph Caldecott (1846-1886) produced sixty-two picture books altogether, and they were immensely popular.

Kate Greenaway's success surpassed that of Crane and Caldecott, and in 1878 the 20,000 copies of her book *Under the Window* sold out so fast that before the publisher could issue a second printing the first copies were reselling at inflated prices. Her popularity spread from England to the United States, France, and Belgium. Soon the Greenaway rage resulted in clothes, dolls, dishes, vases, and even wallpaper based on her sweet old-fashioned but original designs.

Robert Louis Stevenson looked at *Kate Greenaway's Birthday Book for Children* (1880) and remarked, "These are rather nice rhymes, and I don't think they would be very difficult to do." So from 1881 to 1884 he tried his hand at little rhymes for children, and they were printed in 1885 as *A Child's Garden of Verses.* Stevenson had hoped to have this book illustrated by Caldecott, Crane, or Greenaway; but they were not available. His verses were published with no illustrations at all, and people loved them anyway.

At last, in this edition, Stevenson's verses for children appear with art by his chosen illustrators Walter Crane and Kate Greenaway. This is art that they produced for other books of Stevenson's day.

As Kate Greenaway aged, she remarked, "I go on liking things more and more, seeing them more and more beautiful." Her famous friend John Ruskin told her she was "a mixed child and woman," because of her childlike wonder. Walter Crane wrote on that very subject, "It appears to me that there is a certain receptive impressionable quality of mind, whether in young or old, which we call child-like. A fresh direct vision, a quickly stimulated imagination, a love of symbolic and typical form, with a touch of poetic suggestion, a delight in frank gay colour, and a sensitiveness to the variations of line, and contrasts of form—these are some of the characteristics of the child, whether grown up or not. Happy are they who remain children in these respects through life."

I have made clear again for today's children, grown up or not, words and phrases that became obscure in the passing of a hundred years. Moreover, I added a Christian perspective to every poem. Some verses are much as Stevenson wrote them, and others are drastically changed. I urge everyone to read Stevenson's originals, available in any library, in order to know their nostalgia, delicate humor, and wry sweetness "unbaptized."

My hope is that if Robert Louis Stevenson read these adaptations of his verses he could still say of them, as he did a century ago, "They seem to me to smile, to have a kind of childish treble note that sounds in my ears freshly—not song, if you will, but a child's voice."

Kathryn Lindskoog

Kathryn
Lindskoog, 1982

PART ONE:

Little Children

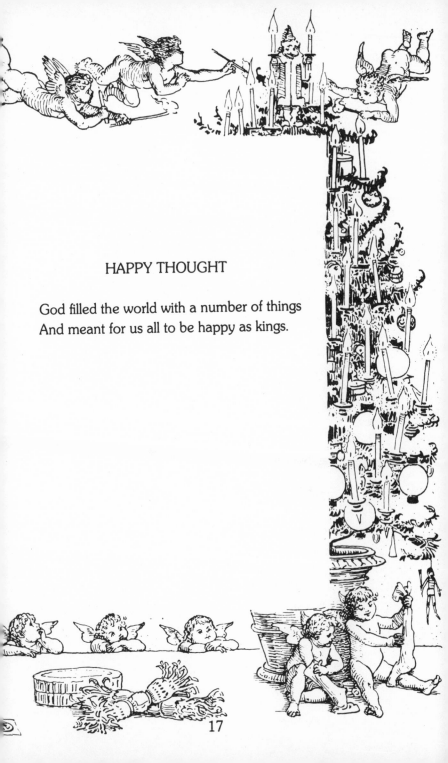

HAPPY THOUGHT

God filled the world with a number of things
And meant for us all to be happy as kings.

18

TO ANY READER

As from your house your mother sees
You playing round the garden trees,
So you may see, if you will look
Through the windows of this book,
Other children far away
As they sleep and rise and play.
Some are very much like you
In how they feel and what they do.

All of us have things to give,
Things to learn and ways to live;
And when all is said and done,
Jesus loves us, every one.

LOOKING FORWARD

When I am grown up tall and straight
I shall be very good and great,
And tell the other girls and boys
That I have learned to share my toys.

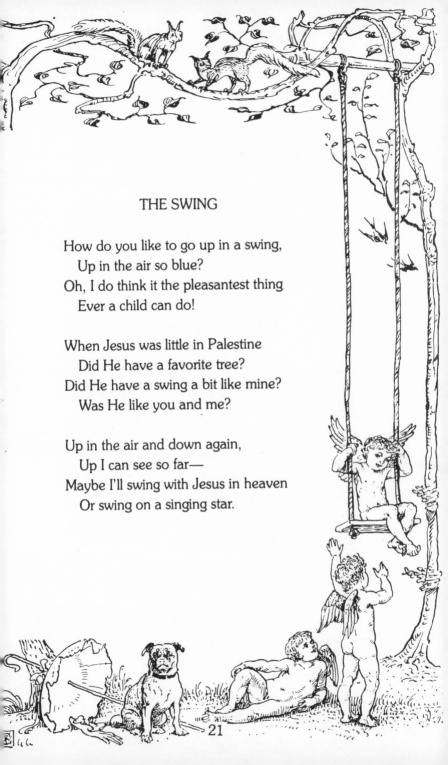

THE SWING

How do you like to go up in a swing,
   Up in the air so blue?
Oh, I do think it the pleasantest thing
   Ever a child can do!

When Jesus was little in Palestine
   Did He have a favorite tree?
Did He have a swing a bit like mine?
   Was He like you and me?

Up in the air and down again,
   Up I can see so far—
Maybe I'll swing with Jesus in heaven
   Or swing on a singing star.

THOUGHT

It would be very nice to think
The world is full of food and drink,
With little children saying grace
In every Christian kind of place.

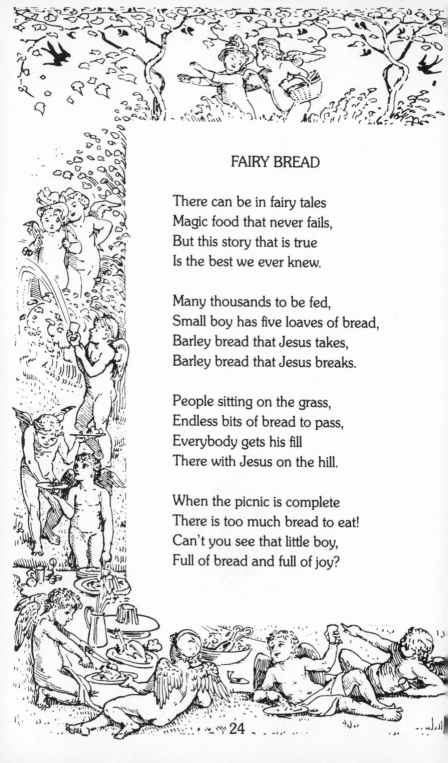

FAIRY BREAD

There can be in fairy tales
Magic food that never fails,
But this story that is true
Is the best we ever knew.

Many thousands to be fed,
Small boy has five loaves of bread,
Barley bread that Jesus takes,
Barley bread that Jesus breaks.

People sitting on the grass,
Endless bits of bread to pass,
Everybody gets his fill
There with Jesus on the hill.

When the picnic is complete
There is too much bread to eat!
Can't you see that little boy,
Full of bread and full of joy?

WHOLE DUTY OF CHILDREN

A child should always say what's true
    And kindly speak when spoken to.
Be mannerly at church and table—
    At least as far as you are able.

K.G

GOOD AND BAD CHILDREN

Children, you are very little
And your bones are not yet brittle;
If you would grow great and stately,
Do not always walk sedately.

Sometimes lively, sometimes quiet,
Be content with healthful diet.
Always do your best to mind;
Concentrate on being kind.

Happy hearts and happy faces,
Happy play in grassy places—
That was how, by ancient means,
Children grew to kings and queens.

But the unkind little prigs,
Those who gobble slop like pigs,
They must never hope for glory—
Theirs is quite a different story!

Cruel children are not nice
And they don't take good advice—
Hated, as the years advance,
By their uncles and their aunts.

Little children, if you would
Grow up kind and safe and good,
Pray to Jesus to be blest—
He knows most and loves the best.

SYSTEM

The child that is not clean and neat,
Who has few toys and things to eat,
He is a needy child, I'm sure—
I think his parents must be poor.

I get my dinner every day,
And every night my prayers I say.
I thank God then and try to care,
And when I'm big enough I'll share.

FOREIGN CHILDREN

Little Swede or Filipino,
Little frosty Eskimo,
Little Chinese folk who please us,
Have you heard about Lord Jesus?

You have seen the northern lights
And the panthers having fights.
You have eaten ostrich eggs
And watched the panda stretch its legs.

Such a life is very fine,
But it's not at all like mine.
To me it isn't very clear
Why it is you don't live here.

You have to live beyond the sea
And cannot come to visit me.
Though I don't know the words you say
I wish that you could come to play.

Little Mexican or Zulu
In Malay or Honolulu,
Little foreign folk who please us,
Have you heard about Lord Jesus?

THE UNSEEN PLAYMATE

When children are playing alone on the green,
Someone is with them who never is seen.
When children are happy and feel understood,
The Friend of the children is doing them good.

Nobody heard Him and nobody saw,
His is a picture you never could draw,
But He's always present, away or at home,
When children are happy and playing alone.

When you feel alone and wish someone were
    there
The Friend of the children will know it and care.
When you feel quite happy and cannot tell why,
The Friend of the children is sure to be by!

'Tis He, when at night you go off to your bed,
Helps you to sleep when you lay down your head.
Our helper in trouble, our Friend when we play,
Jesus is with us at night and all day.

PART TWO:

Let's
Pretend

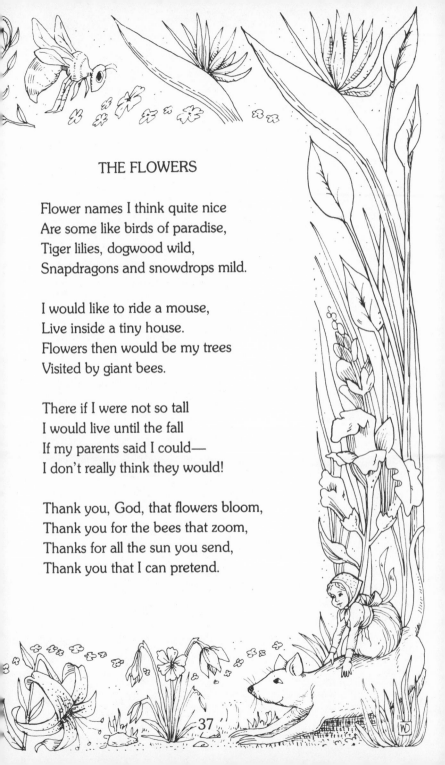

THE FLOWERS

Flower names I think quite nice
Are some like birds of paradise,
Tiger lilies, dogwood wild,
Snapdragons and snowdrops mild.

I would like to ride a mouse,
Live inside a tiny house.
Flowers then would be my trees
Visited by giant bees.

There if I were not so tall
I would live until the fall
If my parents said I could—
I don't really think they would!

Thank you, God, that flowers bloom,
Thank you for the bees that zoom,
Thanks for all the sun you send,
Thank you that I can pretend.

MY SHIP AND I

O it's I that am the captain of a tiny little ship,
  Of a ship that goes a-sailing on the pond;
And my ship it keeps a-turning all around and all
      about;
But when I'm a little older I shall find the secret out
  How to send my boat much straighter on
      beyond.

For I plan to shrink as little as the sailor at the
      helm,
  And the sailor toy I plan to make alive;
And with him beside to help me, it's a-sailing I shall
      go,

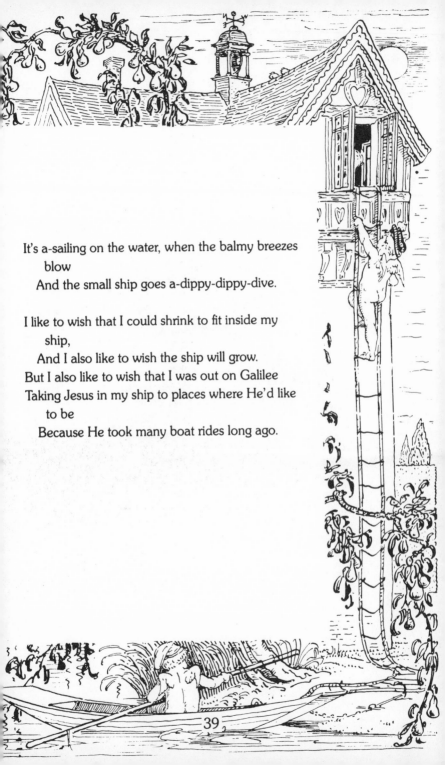

It's a-sailing on the water, when the balmy breezes
    blow
    And the small ship goes a-dippy-dippy-dive.

I like to wish that I could shrink to fit inside my
    ship,
    And I also like to wish the ship will grow.
But I also like to wish that I was out on Galilee
Taking Jesus in my ship to places where He'd like
    to be
    Because He took many boat rides long ago.

GOOD PLAY

We built a ship upon the stairs,
All made of back bedroom chairs,
And filled it full of sofa cushions
To go a-sailing on the oceans.

We left Jerusalem at noon,
Taking two apples and a spoon.
We took a Bible, to be sure,
And we were ready to endure
Whatever perils might befall
God's heroes, Barnabas and Paul.

We sailed along day after day
And preached the Word along the way.
But Paul fell out and hurt his knee,
So there was no one left but me.

THE LAND OF COUNTERPANE

When I was sick and lay abed,
I had two pillows at my head,
And all my toys beside me lay
To keep me happy all the day.

I had my trees and houses out
And planted cities all about,
Across the mountains and the plain
In bedspread-land called Counterpane.

42

And sometimes for an hour or so
I watched the animals all go
Among the blankets to the ark,
Where Noah waited to embark.

And then the water came in sheets
And swept away the towns and streets,
But on my knees old Noah's boat
Rocked on the sheets and stayed afloat.

THE LITTLE LAND

When at home alone I sit
And get very tired of it,
I just have to shut my eyes
To go sailing through the skies—
To go sailing far away
To my special Land of Play;
To the happy land afar
Where we tiny people are;
Where the clover tops are trees,
And the puddles are the seas,
And the leaves, like little ships,
Sail about on tiny trips;
And above the daisy tree
    Through the grasses,
Far above the bumblebee
    Hums and passes.

In that forest where I go
I can see some friends I know—
See the spider and the fly,
And the ants go marching by
Carrying things with their feet
Down the green and grassy street.
I can climb the uncut grass
    And on high
See the great big birds fly past
    In the sky,
And the round sun high and free—
They would never notice me!

45

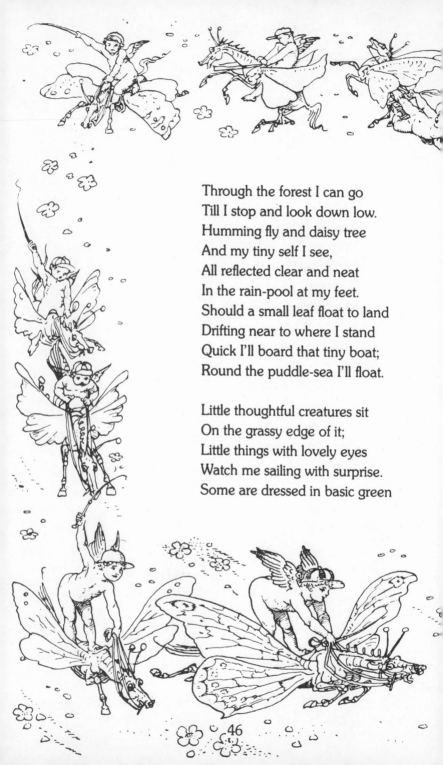

Through the forest I can go
Till I stop and look down low.
Humming fly and daisy tree
And my tiny self I see,
All reflected clear and neat
In the rain-pool at my feet.
Should a small leaf float to land
Drifting near to where I stand
Quick I'll board that tiny boat;
Round the puddle-sea I'll float.

Little thoughtful creatures sit
On the grassy edge of it;
Little things with lovely eyes
Watch me sailing with surprise.
Some are dressed in basic green

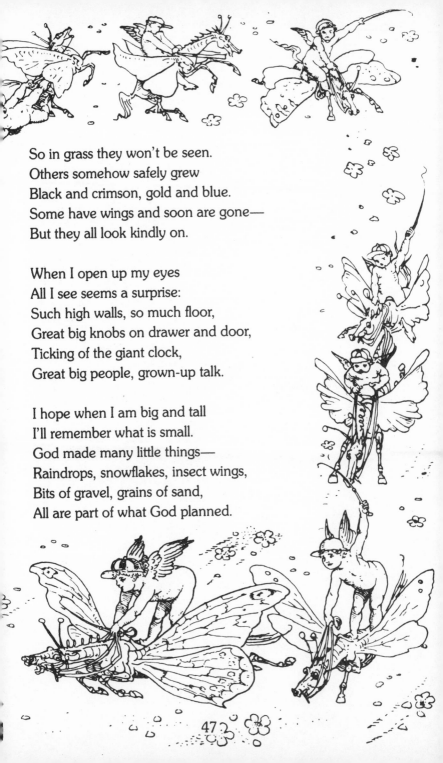

So in grass they won't be seen.
Others somehow safely grew
Black and crimson, gold and blue.
Some have wings and soon are gone—
But they all look kindly on.

When I open up my eyes
All I see seems a surprise:
Such high walls, so much floor,
Great big knobs on drawer and door,
Ticking of the giant clock,
Great big people, grown-up talk.

I hope when I am big and tall
I'll remember what is small.
God made many little things—
Raindrops, snowflakes, insect wings,
Bits of gravel, grains of sand,
All are part of what God planned.

THE LAND OF STORYBOOKS

At evening when the lamp is lit
My parents often sit and sit.
They often talk on everything
But do not play at anything.

Now, on my hands and knees I crawl
All in the dark along the wall,
And follow round the forest track
Away behind the sofa back.

There in the night where none can spy
All in my shepherd's cave I lie
And play at stories that I know
Before it's off to bed I go.

These are the hills, these are the rocks,
Where I am guarding sheep in flocks,
And there the river by whose brink
The roaring lions come to drink.

I'm not afraid of lion claws,
I'm not afraid of big bear paws.
While other people talk or sleep
I play my harp and save my sheep.

Then I am called away to bed
Like any other sleepyhead;
But I was David for a while,
And playing David makes me smile.

HISTORICAL ASSOCIATIONS

Please come with me. Our yard around
   Is not just ordinary ground.
Here many famous deeds were done
   And many battles lost and won.

Perhaps it's best if you are led
   While I for safety march ahead,
For this is somewhat unsafe land—
   So I will lead you by the hand.

Here is the sand, here is the sea,
   Here are the mountains by your knee.
Here was Daniel's lions' den,
   Here came a Good Samaritan.

Here Moses freed the many slaves
   And evil men were drowned by waves.
Here Noah landed on dry land—
   And here a temple used to stand.

Here was a garden and a snake,
   And Paul came here for all our sake.
This is a game I like to play,
   Pretending they were here this way.

Please come with me and walk around
   On all my Bible history ground.
Here many famous deeds were done
   And we can name them and have fun.

BLOCK CITY

What are you able to build with your blocks?
Castles and palaces, temples and docks.
Some people travel to Paris or Rome,
But I can be happy and building at home.

Let the sofa be mountains, the carpet be sea,
There I'll establish a city for me:
A church and a store and a garden beside,
And a stable as well for the horses we ride.

Great is the palace with pillar and wall,
A sort of a tower on top of it all,
And steps coming down in an orderly way
To where my toy ships snuggle safe in the bay.

This ship is sailing and that one is moored:
Listen to songs of the sailors on board!
And see, on the steps of the palace, my kings
Coming and going with presents and things!

Now I am done with it, down let it go!
All in a moment the town is laid low.
Block after block lying scattered and free,
What is there left of my town by the sea?

Block City, Block City, always it falls!
Jericho crashed once and down came the walls.
Many large cities are lost in the past,
But God's holy city in heaven will last.

God's holy city is bright like a crown,
God's holy city will never fall down.
We will all live there and no one will die,
And all will be happy and no one will cry!

THE SILENT SOLDIER

I have a soldier whom I send
On many trips that we pretend.
He goes to war and then comes back
But never talks about attack.

I sent him off to Egypt land
To help the Pharaoh cross the sand
When they were hunting Moses down—
He's lucky that he didn't drown.

I sent him off to Jericho
To help them fight against the foe,

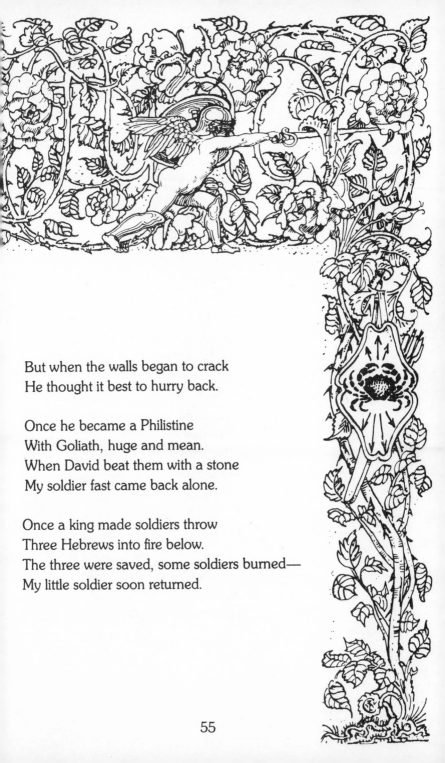

But when the walls began to crack
He thought it best to hurry back.

Once he became a Philistine
With Goliath, huge and mean.
When David beat them with a stone
My soldier fast came back alone.

Once a king made soldiers throw
Three Hebrews into fire below.
The three were saved, some soldiers burned—
My little soldier soon returned.

Peter was in jail, no key,
And an angel set him free!
Soldier guards would pay
   the price—
Mine came home to where
   it's nice.

My soldier goes on story tasks,
He never argues, never asks.
He can fight for bad or good,
He is only made of wood.

Not a word will he disclose,
Not a word of all he knows.
I must lay him on the shelf
And make up his tales myself.

MARCHING SONG

Bring a broom and pans of metal,
   Marching, here we come!
Willie booms on an old kettle,
   Johnnie beats the drum.

Mary Jane commands the marchers,
   Peter's horn will blow.
Feet in time, alert the archers,
   Off to Jericho!

All in military manner,
   Marching double-quick;
While a scarf just like a banner
   Waves upon a stick.

Now the mighty walls are broken.
   Great commander Jane!
With congratulations spoken,
   Let's go home again.

ARMIES IN THE FIRE

The lights now glitter down the street;
Faintly sound the falling feet.
And the evening slowly falls
About the garden trees and walls.

As shadows darken into gloom,
Our fireplace lights the family room
And warmly on the ceiling looks
And flickers on the backs of books.

I see cities in the fire
As the embers blaze up higher.
Down the red-hot valley, oh!
Imaginary armies go!

Blinking embers, tell me true,
Where are those armies marching to?
Are they like the angel guard
That saved Elisha once for God?

The Bible says one evil night
Syria's army came to fight,
But wise Elisha had no fear—
He saw an angel army near.

The angel army blazed with light
Upon the mountains, fiery bright.
So not a person died that day;
The enemies were sent away!

I like to look at flicker flames
And play lots of pretending games.
I think of stories old and new;
Some are made up and some are true!

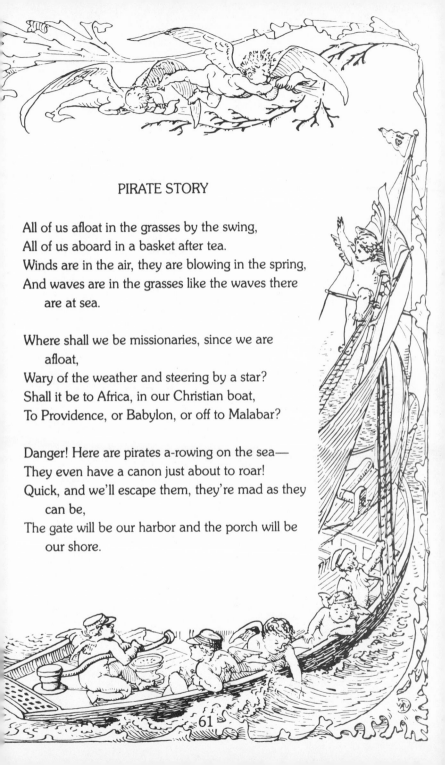

PIRATE STORY

All of us afloat in the grasses by the swing,
All of us aboard in a basket after tea.
Winds are in the air, they are blowing in the spring,
And waves are in the grasses like the waves there
     are at sea.

Where shall we be missionaries, since we are
     afloat,
Wary of the weather and steering by a star?
Shall it be to Africa, in our Christian boat,
To Providence, or Babylon, or off to Malabar?

Danger! Here are pirates a-rowing on the sea—
They even have a canon just about to roar!
Quick, and we'll escape them, they're mad as they
     can be,
The gate will be our harbor and the porch will be
     our shore.

PART THREE:

Seasons
and
Weather

RAIN

God's rain is falling all around,
It falls on field and tree,
It rains on the umbrellas here,
And on the ships at sea.

THE WIND

I saw you toss the kites on high
And blow the birds about the sky;
And all around I heard you pass,
Like ladies' skirts across the grass—
   O wind, a-blowing all day long,
   O wind, that sings so loud a song!

I saw the different things you did,
But always you yourself you hid.
I felt you push, I heard you call,
I could not see yourself at all—
   O wind, a-blowing all day long,
   O wind, that sings so loud a song!

The love of God is like the wind.
It tugs at me when I have sinned;
It gives me joy when I've been good.
I'd be God's windmill if I could!
   O wind, a-blowing all day long,
   O wind, that sings so loud a song!

SUMMER SUN

Great is the sun and slowly flies
　　Across our empty open skies.
In all the blue and glowing days
　　He showers us with shiny rays.

Though all the drapes and shades we pull
　　To keep our house a little cool,
Yet he will find a crack or two
　　To slip his golden fingers through.

With his golden face so round
　　He smiles on all the garden ground.
This gardener of the world will glow
　　To please the plants and make them grow.

God showers us with golden love,
　　Far better than the sun above.
Great is our God for it was He
　　Made sun and earth and sky and sea!

WINTERTIME

Late lies the wintry sun abed,
Much like a lazy sleepyhead;
A few cold hours up; and then,
How soon the low sun sets again.

When I go out to look around
And walk across the frozen ground
The cold wind burns my face and blows
Its frosty pepper up my nose.

Black are my steps on silver snow;
White is the frosty breath I blow;
And tree and house, and hill and lake,
Are frosted like a birthday cake.

Our favorite birthday of the year
Arrives when icy winter's here.
Then we have special songs and play,
For Christ was born on Christmas day.

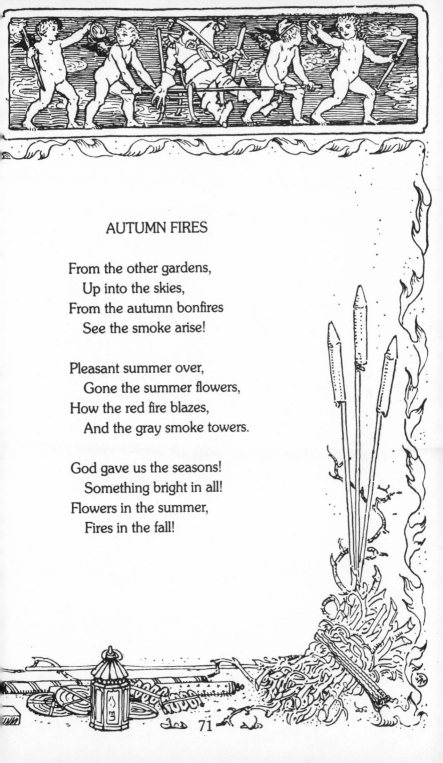

AUTUMN FIRES

From the other gardens,
  Up into the skies,
From the autumn bonfires
  See the smoke arise!

Pleasant summer over,
  Gone the summer flowers,
How the red fire blazes,
  And the gray smoke towers.

God gave us the seasons!
  Something bright in all!
Flowers in the summer,
  Fires in the fall!

SINGING

Of speckled eggs the wild bird sings,
　　And nests among the trees;
The sailor sings of ropes and things
　　In ships upon the seas.

The children sing in far Japan,
　　The children sing in Spain;
The angels sing in Godlight
　　While we're singing in the rain.

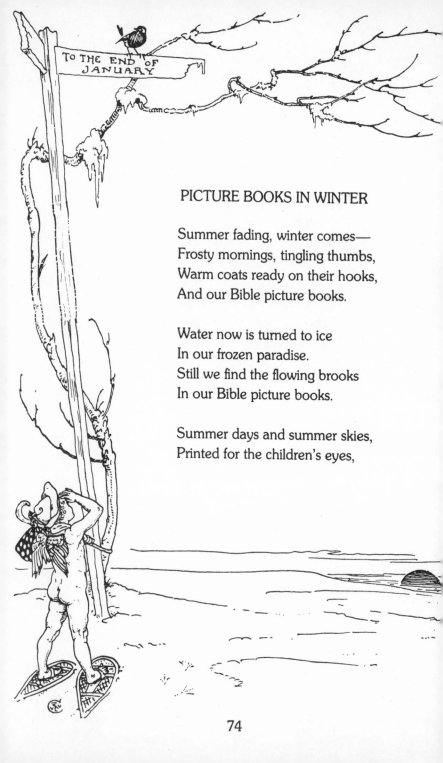

PICTURE BOOKS IN WINTER

Summer fading, winter comes—
Frosty mornings, tingling thumbs,
Warm coats ready on their hooks,
And our Bible picture books.

Water now is turned to ice
In our frozen paradise.
Still we find the flowing brooks
In our Bible picture books.

Summer days and summer skies,
Printed for the children's eyes,

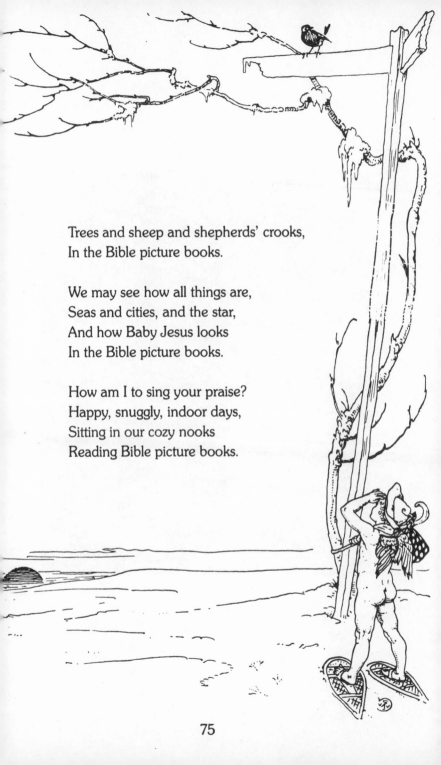

Trees and sheep and shepherds' crooks,
In the Bible picture books.

We may see how all things are,
Seas and cities, and the star,
And how Baby Jesus looks
In the Bible picture books.

How am I to sing your praise?
Happy, snuggly, indoor days,
Sitting in our cozy nooks
Reading Bible picture books.

NEST EGGS

Birds all the summer day
   Flutter and quarrel
Here in the tree they love
   We call a laurel.

Here in the fork
   The brown nest is seated;
Four little blue eggs
   The mother keeps heated.

Safe in each egg
   Babies are growing.
Inside the eggshells
   Babies aren't showing.

When eggshells crack,
   Birdies a-springing
Make all the April woods
   Merry with singing.

We with our wisdom
   And sensible talking
While they fly overhead
   Still will be walking.

* * * *

Jesus said God knows
   Every small bird,
And we can trust
   In Jesus' word.

Jesus says God knows
   Birds in the wild;
Jesus says God loves
   Every child.

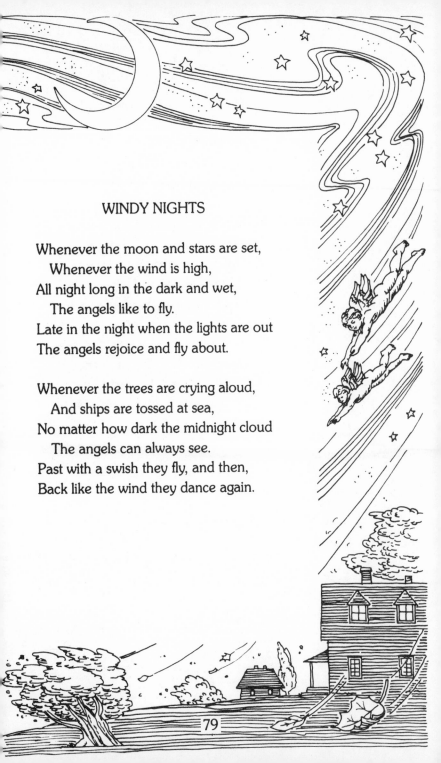

WINDY NIGHTS

Whenever the moon and stars are set,
   Whenever the wind is high,
All night long in the dark and wet,
   The angels like to fly.
Late in the night when the lights are out
The angels rejoice and fly about.

Whenever the trees are crying aloud,
   And ships are tossed at sea,
No matter how dark the midnight cloud
   The angels can always see.
Past with a swish they fly, and then,
Back like the wind they dance again.

THE COW

The friendly cow all brown and white,
  I love with all my heart.
I think that when God made the cow
  He made her part by part.
At giving milk she's dutiful;
  Her moo is loud and funny;
Her eyes are big and beautiful;
  Her nose is wet and runny.
Her tongue is large and very rough;
  Her tail is quick and whisky;
Her hoofs are very hard and tough;
  Her ears are furry-frisky.
Yet blown by all the winds that pass
  And wet with all the showers,
She walks among the meadow grass
  And eats the meadow flowers.

PART FOUR:

Special
Places

AT THE SEASHORE

When I was down beside God's sea,
A little spade they gave to me
   To dig the sandy shore.

My holes were empty like a cup.
But like God's love the sea came up
   Till they could hold no more.

FAREWELL TO THE FARM

The car is at the door at last;
The eager children climb in fast
And all their happy voices ring,
Good-bye, good-bye, to everything!

To house and garden, field and lawn,
The meadow-gates we swung upon,
To pump and stable, tree and swing,
Good-bye, good-bye, to everything!

And fare you well for evermore,
O ladder at the hayloft door,
O hayloft where the cobwebs cling,
Good-bye, good-bye, to everything.

Our visit's over; off we go.
The trees and houses smaller grow;
Last, round the woody turn we swing:
We thank you, God, for everything!

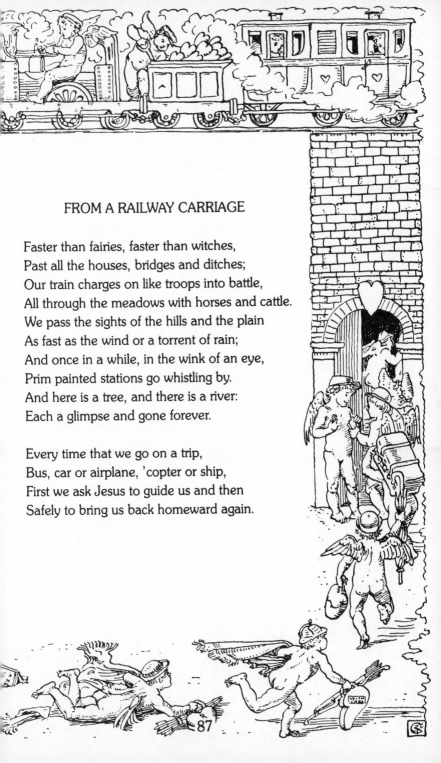

FROM A RAILWAY CARRIAGE

Faster than fairies, faster than witches,
Past all the houses, bridges and ditches;
Our train charges on like troops into battle,
All through the meadows with horses and cattle.
We pass the sights of the hills and the plain
As fast as the wind or a torrent of rain;
And once in a while, in the wink of an eye,
Prim painted stations go whistling by.
And here is a tree, and there is a river:
Each a glimpse and gone forever.

Every time that we go on a trip,
Bus, car or airplane, 'copter or ship,
First we ask Jesus to guide us and then
Safely to bring us back homeward again.

MY KINGDOM

Down by a shining water pool
I found a place all green and cool,
    No higher than my head.
The flower bushes all about
In summer bloom were coming out,
    Some yellow and some red.

I called the little pool a sea;
The little hills were big to me,
    For I am very small.
I made a boat, I made a town,
I ran some roadways up and down,
    And named them one and all.

And all about was mine, I said,
The little sparrows overhead,
    The water minnows too.

This was the world and I was king;
For me the birds came by to sing,
  For me the insects flew.

I played there were no deeper seas,
Nor any wider plains than these,
  No other kings but me.
At last I heard my mother call—
The world was larger after all!
  I hurried home for tea.

I loved my kingdom, small and sweet,
That spread about my busy feet
  When I was playing king.
Does God love the huge world He made
The way I loved the place I played?
  He must love everything.

KEEPSAKE MILL

Here is the mill with the humming of thunder,
  Here is the stream with the wonder of foam,
Here is the drain with the race running under—
  Marvelous flour mill near my old home.

Down by the banks of the river it rattled,
  Turning the grain into flour to cook,
Grinding it fine. And nobody tattled
  When village children went there to look.

Sounds of the village grew stiller and stiller,
  Stiller the notes of the birds on the hill.
Dusty and dim were the eyes of the miller,
  Deaf were his ears in the roar of the mill.

Years have gone by. Does the wheel in the river
   Wheel as it wheeled for us, children, today?
Wheel and keep roaring and foaming forever,
   Long after children grow up and away?

Mills by the hundreds were built to grind flour,
   People for centuries built all the mills.
God made the people and gave them the power—
   God made the streams and the village and hills.

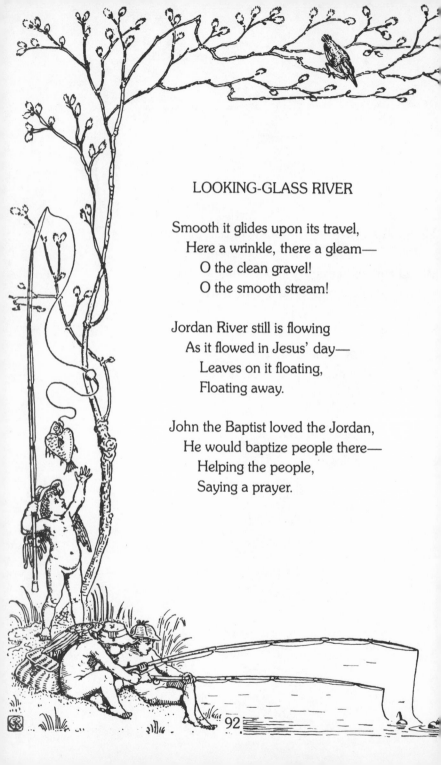

LOOKING-GLASS RIVER

Smooth it glides upon its travel,
    Here a wrinkle, there a gleam—
        O the clean gravel!
        O the smooth stream!

Jordan River still is flowing
    As it flowed in Jesus' day—
        Leaves on it floating,
        Floating away.

John the Baptist loved the Jordan,
    He would baptize people there—
        Helping the people,
        Saying a prayer.

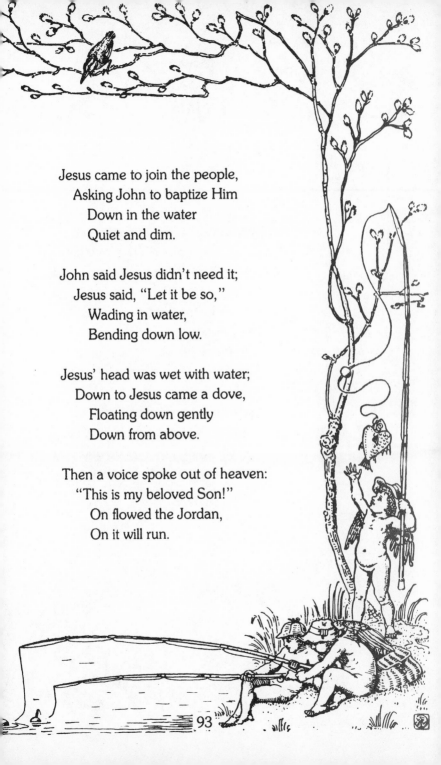

Jesus came to join the people,
Asking John to baptize Him
Down in the water
Quiet and dim.

John said Jesus didn't need it;
Jesus said, "Let it be so,"
Wading in water,
Bending down low.

Jesus' head was wet with water;
Down to Jesus came a dove,
Floating down gently
Down from above.

Then a voice spoke out of heaven:
"This is my beloved Son!"
On flowed the Jordan,
On it will run.

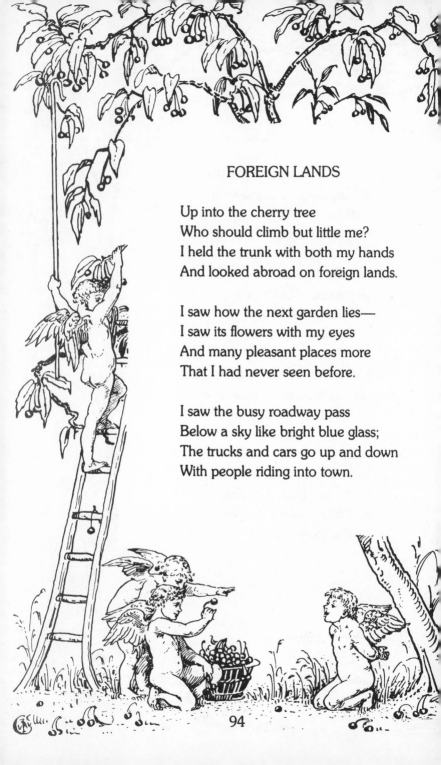

FOREIGN LANDS

Up into the cherry tree
Who should climb but little me?
I held the trunk with both my hands
And looked abroad on foreign lands.

I saw how the next garden lies—
I saw its flowers with my eyes
And many pleasant places more
That I had never seen before.

I saw the busy roadway pass
Below a sky like bright blue glass;
The trucks and cars go up and down
With people riding into town.

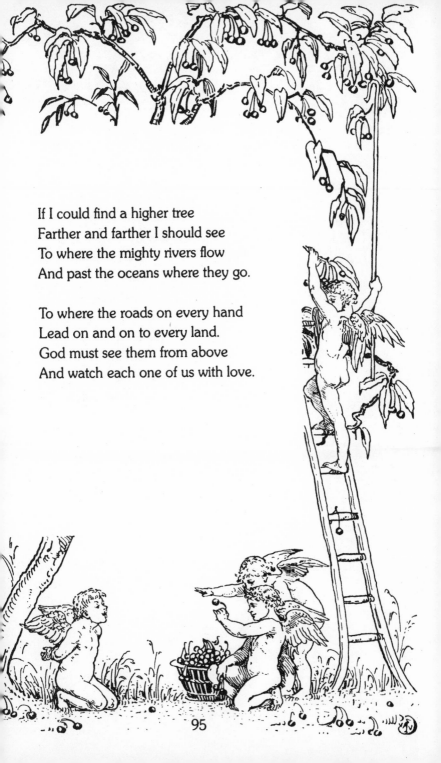

If I could find a higher tree
Farther and farther I should see
To where the mighty rivers flow
And past the oceans where they go.

To where the roads on every hand
Lead on and on to every land.
God must see them from above
And watch each one of us with love.

TRAVEL

I should like to rise and go
Where the golden apples grow,
Where below another sky
Bible countries somewhere lie.
I would see Jerusalem
And all the lands of Abraham.

I would like to make my way
From Israel to far Cathay.
There I'd see the China Wall
And walk along its top so tall.

Then I think it would be nice
To trudge across some arctic ice,
Seeking out the polar bear
And people in their igloos there.

Where snow is just a melted dream
And forests feel like steamy steam,
Full of apes and coconuts
And some missionary huts—
Where the knotty crocodile
Lies and blinks beside the Nile
And the red flamingo flies,
Seeking fish with eager eyes—
There in jungles green and great
Man-devouring tigers wait,
Lying close with anxious ear
Lest the hunters come too near.

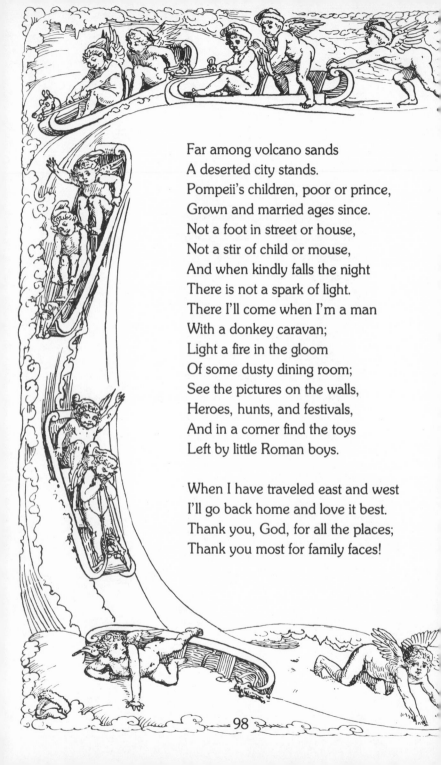

Far among volcano sands
A deserted city stands.
Pompeii's children, poor or prince,
Grown and married ages since.
Not a foot in street or house,
Not a stir of child or mouse,
And when kindly falls the night
There is not a spark of light.
There I'll come when I'm a man
With a donkey caravan;
Light a fire in the gloom
Of some dusty dining room;
See the pictures on the walls,
Heroes, hunts, and festivals,
And in a corner find the toys
Left by little Roman boys.

When I have traveled east and west
I'll go back home and love it best.
Thank you, God, for all the places;
Thank you most for family faces!

WHERE GO THE BOATS?

Dark brown is the river,
  Golden is the sand.
It seems to flow forever,
  With trees on either hand.

On goes the river
  Away down the hill.
Away down the valley,
  My boat's on it still.

Green leaves a-floating
  Show me God's care.
When I play boating
  I whisper a prayer.

Away down the river
  A hundred miles or more,
Other little children
  May bring my boats ashore.

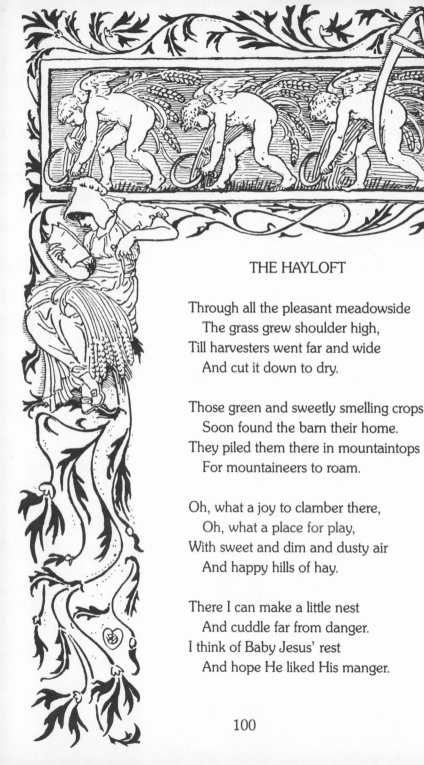

THE HAYLOFT

Through all the pleasant meadowside
  The grass grew shoulder high,
Till harvesters went far and wide
  And cut it down to dry.

Those green and sweetly smelling crops
  Soon found the barn their home.
They piled them there in mountaintops
  For mountaineers to roam.

Oh, what a joy to clamber there,
  Oh, what a place for play,
With sweet and dim and dusty air
  And happy hills of hay.

There I can make a little nest
  And cuddle far from danger.
I think of Baby Jesus' rest
  And hope He liked His manger.

PART FIVE:

Special
People

TO MY NAME-CHILD

Some day this book of jingles, if you learn to read
    with speed,
My dear little Fay Ellen, will be given you to read.
Then shall you discover that your name was
    printed down
By the busy, busy printers, long before, in some far
    town.

Near a great and busy city where the east and west
    are met
All the busy letters by the busy printer set.
While you thought of little and were busy with your
    play,
Busy grown-ups thought of you in places far away.

Yes, and while you took your nap, perhaps in
    other lands,
Other little children took the verses in their hands.
Other children questioned, because questions
    seem to tease:
"Who is little Fay here, won't you tell us, Mother,
    please?"

KC

Now that you have read this jingle, lay it down and
    play
With your Pasadena playmates if it is a sunny day,
Planning trips to Disneyland and other things that
    please
Little girls in cities near the huge Pacific seas.

And remember in your playing, when this verse is
    through,
Long before you knew it, how I told you what to
    do.
While you knew me only as a lady you called Kay.
I was praying fondly for my godchild little Fay.

TO AUNTIE

Best of all aunts, not only I,
But all the family children sigh—
What do other children do?
God was so kind to give me you!

THE LAMPLIGHTER

Tom wants to be a driver and Maria's off to sea,
And Papa is a banker and as rich as he can be;
But I, when I am stronger and can choose what I'm
to do,
I'd like to work the power plant and light the lamps
for you.

When evening is ready and the sun has left the sky
It's time to watch the streetlights turn on suddenly
up high.
No one seems to touch them, and I often wonder
which
Man or woman far away so kindly works the
switch.

It's good to have the lights go on so I can see the
street;
Somebody helps the lights go on to safely guide
our feet.
Once all the world was wild and dark and
everything was night,
But God had all the power and He first turned on
the light.

MY TREASURES

These nuts, that I keep at the back of the nest
Where all of my marbles are lying at rest,
Were gathered in autumn by Mother and me
In a wood with a well by the side of the sea.

This whistle we made (and how clearly it sounds!)
By the side of a field at the end of the grounds,
From the branch of a tree, with a knife of my own.
It was Father who made it, and Father alone.

The stone, with the white and the yellow and gray,
We discovered I cannot tell *how* far away;
And I carried it back although weary and cold,
For though Father denies it, I'm sure it is gold.

Of all of my treasures the last is a book—
Although I can't read it, I turn it and look.
It is a Bible they gave me to hold;
I'll read every page when I get big and old.

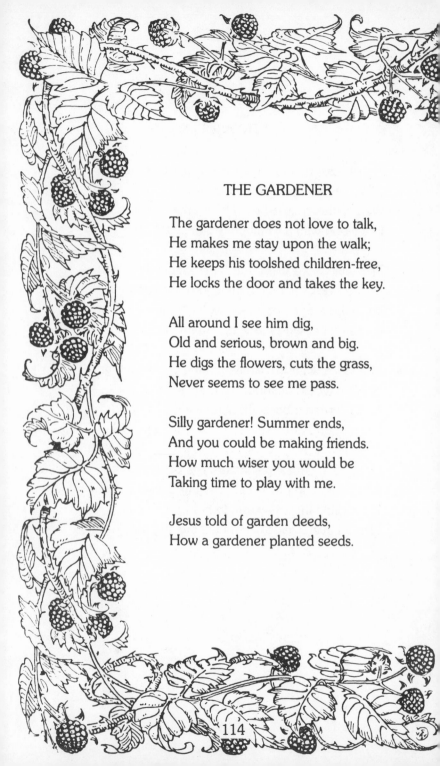

THE GARDENER

The gardener does not love to talk,
He makes me stay upon the walk;
He keeps his toolshed children-free,
He locks the door and takes the key.

All around I see him dig,
Old and serious, brown and big.
He digs the flowers, cuts the grass,
Never seems to see me pass.

Silly gardener! Summer ends,
And you could be making friends.
How much wiser you would be
Taking time to play with me.

Jesus told of garden deeds,
How a gardener planted seeds.

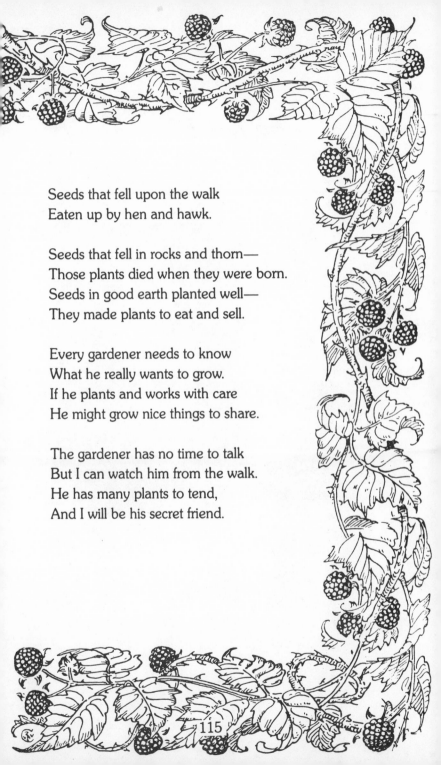

Seeds that fell upon the walk
Eaten up by hen and hawk.

Seeds that fell in rocks and thorn—
Those plants died when they were born.
Seeds in good earth planted well—
They made plants to eat and sell.

Every gardener needs to know
What he really wants to grow.
If he plants and works with care
He might grow nice things to share.

The gardener has no time to talk
But I can watch him from the walk.
He has many plants to tend,
And I will be his secret friend.

AUNTIE'S SKIRTS

Whenever Auntie's skirts are long
They make a kind of swishing song.
They whisper like my angel's wings
And make me think of lovely things.

TO MY MOTHER

You too, my mother, read these rhymes
And cherish these God-given times.
Surely the rhymes that please you more
Are my small footsteps on the floor.

TO WILLIE AND HENRIETTA

If two may rightly hear
These rhymes of childhood cheer
And house and garden play
You two, my cousins, and you only, may.

You in a garden green
With me were king and queen,
Were hunter, soldier, star,
And all the thousand things that children are.

Now in our grown-up seat
We rest with quiet feet
And in a grown-up way
We watch the children, all the new ones, play.

Times past seem to be gone
And time keeps moving on;
But we are children still
For God is loving us and always will.

TO ONE WHO CARED FOR ME

For the long nights you lay awake
And watched me closely for my sake,
For your most comfortable hand
That helped me walk and helped me stand,
For all the storybooks you read,
For all the fears you comforted.

For all you praised and pains you bore,
For all your cheer and every chore,
For all your prayers and all my tears—
The angel of my infant years—
For all the special cares you took,
Now take from me this special book.

And grant it, Lord, that all who read
This book may find a friend indeed,
And every child who hears my rhyme,
In happy, cozy storytime,
May hear it in as kind a voice
As made my childhood days rejoice!

TO MINNIE

The big room with the giant bed
Where just our parents laid their head;
The baby room where you and I
Used to go at night to lie.
Room where we would leave our clothes,
Room where grown-up business goes,
Room where we would take our bath,
Room where we had made a path.

I your brother had no fears
We would move in later years.
I would live there all my life;
You would someday be my wife.

The happy playroom, best of all,
With pictures taped up on the wall
And leaves upon the glass—
A pleasant room in which to wake
And hear the leafy garden shake
When breezes chose to pass—
How pleasant there to lie in bed
And see the pictures overhead.

These are vanished clean away
And that house is changed today;
Other people took our place,
Other things fill all the space.

The winding road, the little hill,
Are near our childhood's garden still;
But now we children never more
Will run out through the kitchen door.
I can hear us call and say
When we ran outside to play,
"Hide and seek! Hide and seek!"
Count to ten and do not peek!

You are hid from me, my dear.
I no longer find you here.
Childhood over, sister gone,
Memories to dwell upon.

"Hide and seek! Hide and seek!"
How I'd like to hear you speak.
I would run behind a tree,
Find you hiding there from me.
But I know we'll meet again—
There's no way to tell just when.
In God's garden we will meet,
Loyal brother, sister sweet.

Things won't ever be the same—
They'll be better. In our game
I would call out, "Here I come!"
Life is that adventuresome.

PART SIX:

Bedtime and Wake-up Time

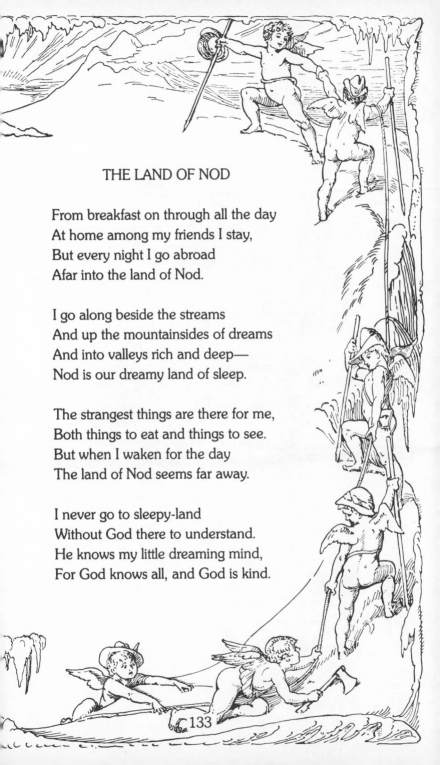

THE LAND OF NOD

From breakfast on through all the day
At home among my friends I stay,
But every night I go abroad
Afar into the land of Nod.

I go along beside the streams
And up the mountainsides of dreams
And into valleys rich and deep—
Nod is our dreamy land of sleep.

The strangest things are there for me,
Both things to eat and things to see.
But when I waken for the day
The land of Nod seems far away.

I never go to sleepy-land
Without God there to understand.
He knows my little dreaming mind,
For God knows all, and God is kind.

MY BED IS A BOAT

My bed is like a little boat
   I sail on in the dark,
Pajamas are my sailor coat—
   I fear no whale or shark.

I say my prayers and then I say
   Good night to friends on shore.
I shut my eyes and sail away
   And see and hear no more.

When Moses was a baby dear
   His mother made a boat.
She tucked him in without a fear
   So he could sleep and float.

His boat was like a little bed,
   And he was safe and sound;
The princess saw him and she said,
   "Come see what I have found!"

So God took care of Moses
   In very special ways,
And everyone supposes
   He was grateful all his days.

THE SUN TRAVELS

The sun is not in bed when I
At night upon my pillow lie
Because a nightly trip he takes
And morning after morning makes.

When every Eastern sleepyhead
Is being kissed and put to bed,
Then all the children in the West
Are getting up and getting dressed.

But God is different from the sun;
His time with us is never done.
He never goes away at night
And we are always in His sight.

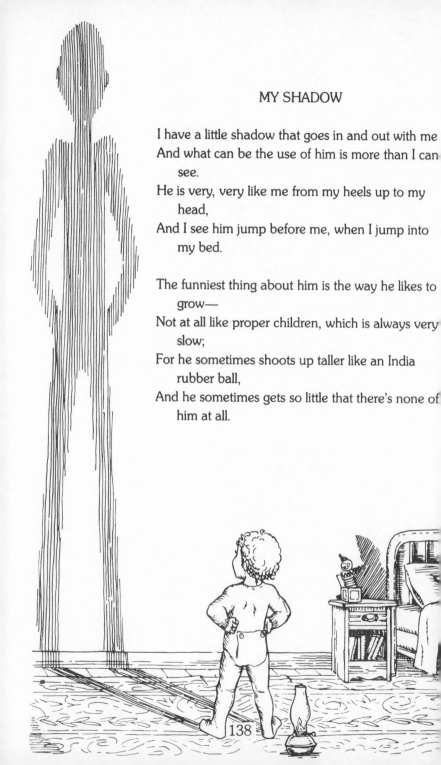

MY SHADOW

I have a little shadow that goes in and out with me
And what can be the use of him is more than I can
    see.
He is very, very like me from my heels up to my
    head,
And I see him jump before me, when I jump into
    my bed.

The funniest thing about him is the way he likes to
    grow—
Not at all like proper children, which is always very
    slow;
For he sometimes shoots up taller like an India
    rubber ball,
And he sometimes gets so little that there's none of
    him at all.

I have a guardian angel who goes in and out with
    me,
And what can be the use of him is very plain to
    see.
He cares so much about me from my heels up to
    my head,
And he is always by me, when I jump into my bed.

I know he's always with me, everywhere I go;
The strangest thing about him is the fact he doesn't
    show.
I think that he is shining and very big and bright,
I think that he is loving and he is always right.

139

GOOD NIGHT

When our bright lamps are turned back on
The sun is setting, then it's gone;
And all outside among the ferns,
The creeping night again returns.

Now we can see the big logs glow
Inside the fireplace bright and low;
My face reflecting as I pass
Like pictures on the window glass.

Does bedtime come so soon tonight?
Let me be brave and do it right
And after my good-nights are said
Then let me hurry off to bed.

Good night, then, Brother, Sister, Dad!
Around the fire you all look glad!
God give you all a pleasant rest
And let our house be safe and blessed.

SHADOW MARCH

All around the house is the jet-black night;
   It spills through the window glass.
It crawls in the corners, away from the light,
   And it follows me as I pass.

Now my little heart's like a beating drum,
   When I feel afraid of the dark;
And while I'm alone I see some shadows come
   And then I hear a far dog bark!

Then I'm glad I know God is watching me
   When I'm going to my bed,
And I picture angels here that I can't see,
   Imagining their soft wings spread.

IN PORT

I patter in and look around—
Everything is safe and sound,
Snug in my warm and cheerful room
Far away from cold and gloom.

Under the covers I climb and pray
And thank God for another day.
I close my sleepy eyes at last—
Another busy day is past.

I know when Mommy goes to bed
She'll come and touch my dreaming head.
She always comes to take a peek
And kiss me on my waiting cheek.

TIME TO RISE

A birdie with a yellow bill
Hopped upon the window sill,
Cocked his shining eye and said:
"God loves you, little sleepyhead!"

YOUNG NIGHT-THOUGHT

Almost every single night
When my mom puts out the light
I pretend that I can see
Bible people visit me.

Armies, wise women and kings
Bringing different kinds of things
And marching in so grand a way
You never saw the like by day.

So fine a show was never seen
Upon a television screen,
For every Bible beast and man
Is marching in that caravan.

At first they move a little slow,
But fast and faster on they go.
We travel down through valleys deep
Until we reach the land of Sleep.

NIGHT AND DAY

When the golden day is done,
  Through the closing gateway
Child and garden, flower, sun
  Vanish in the late day.

As the darkest shadows fall
  As the night is nearing
Under evening's cloak they all
  Soft are disappearing.

Garden darkened, flowers close,
  Children down to slumber.
In the quiet children doze;
  Dreams we cannot number.

In the darkness houses glow;
  Lamps are lit and candles,
Till when all the parents go
  Turn their bedroom handles.

Then at last the day begins
  In the east a-breaking
And the sunlight quickly wins,
  Sleeping birds awaking.

Then the shady shapes so gray
  Start to change to clearness.
Then the feeling far away
  Starts to change to nearness.

I look out my window now,
    See my yard parading.
Just last night I looked at how
    It was dim and fading!

All our lives when we are small
    Evening comes at seven—
But we won't have night at all
    When we get to heaven.

There we'll be with every friend,
    Never ever weeping.
There the days will never end
    And we won't need sleeping.

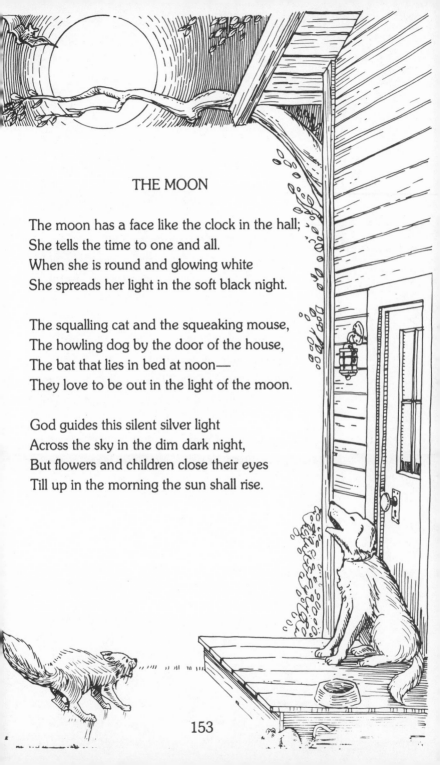

THE MOON

The moon has a face like the clock in the hall;
She tells the time to one and all.
When she is round and glowing white
She spreads her light in the soft black night.

The squalling cat and the squeaking mouse,
The howling dog by the door of the house,
The bat that lies in bed at noon—
They love to be out in the light of the moon.

God guides this silent silver light
Across the sky in the dim dark night,
But flowers and children close their eyes
Till up in the morning the sun shall rise.

153

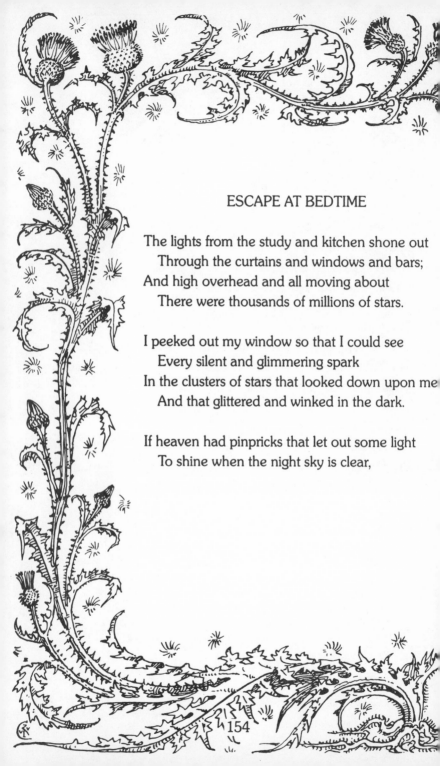

ESCAPE AT BEDTIME

The lights from the study and kitchen shone out
   Through the curtains and windows and bars;
And high overhead and all moving about
   There were thousands of millions of stars.

I peeked out my window so that I could see
   Every silent and glimmering spark
In the clusters of stars that looked down upon me
   And that glittered and winked in the dark.

If heaven had pinpricks that let out some light
   To shine when the night sky is clear,

Then that could account for this glorious sight
    That somehow made heaven seem near.

They saw I was up and exclaimed with surprise
    And they soon had me tucked back in bed,
But the glory kept shining all bright in my eyes,
    And the stars going round in my head.

I wish I had been with the shepherds that night
    Out under the radiant sky,
When one star was glorious, special, and bright,
    And Jesus was born right near by.

A GOOD BOY

I woke before the morning, I was happy all the
    day,
I never said an ugly word, but smiled and stuck to
    play.

And now at last the sun is going down behind the
    wood,
And I am very happy, for I know that I've been
    good.

My bed is waiting cool and fresh, with linens
    smooth and fair

And I must be off to sleepy-by, and not forget my
    prayer.

I pray that, till tomorrow when I see the sun arise,
No ugly dreams shall fright my mind, no ugly sight
    my eyes.

But slumber hold me tightly till I waken in the
    dawn,
And hear the thrushes singing in the lilacs round
    the lawn.

BED IN SUMMER

In winter I get up at night
   And dress by an electric light.
In summer, quite the other way,
   I have to go to bed by day.

I have to go to bed and say
   My goodnight prayer when it is day.
I think it odd to pray at night
   If all the sky is blue and bright.

In summer we have so much sun
   That it is light when day is done.
But dark or light, I kneel and pray,
   And God is with me either way.